This Book Belongs To

Name: _____

Phone: _____

Email: _____

E♭: I   Vi   iii   viiº   V   ii   IV   I   Vi

E f G A B C D
1 2 3 4 5 6 7

A B C D e F G

Vi   iii   IV   I   iii

E f G A B C D
1 2 3 4 5 6 7

COMPLETE MUSIC THEORY GUIDE

Lines

Staff/stave

The five-line staff (often "stave" in British usage) is used to indicate pitch. Each line or space indicates the pitch belonging to a note with a letter name: A, B, C, D, E, F, G. Moving vertically upwards, the letter names proceed alphabetically with the alternating lines and spaces, and represent ascending pitches. The A-G pattern repeats continually—the note above "G" is always another "A". A clef is almost always added, which assigns one specific pitch to one specific line; the other lines and spaces are determined alphabetically as described.

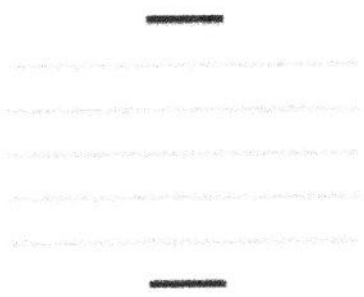

Ledger or leger lines

These additional lines (and the spaces they form) indicate pitches above or below the staff. The diagram shows a single ledger line above and below the staff but multiple ledger lines can be used.

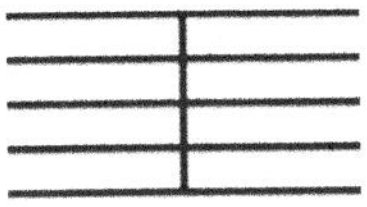

Bar line (or barline)

Bar lines separate measures ("bars") of music according to the indicated time signature. They sometimes extend through multiple staves to group them together when a grand staff is used or when indicating groups of similar instruments in a conductor's score.

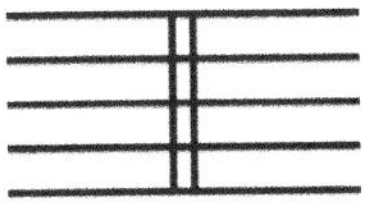

Double bar line

These indicate some change in the music, such as a new musical section, or a new key/time signature.

Bold double bar line

These indicate the conclusion of a movement or composition.

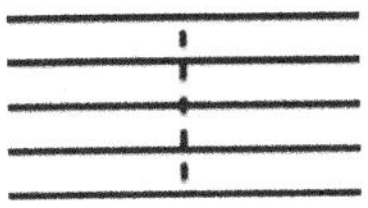

Dotted bar line

These can be used to subdivide measures of complex meter into shorter segments for ease of reading.

Bracket

A bracket is used to connect two or more lines of music that sound simultaneously. In contemporary usage it usually connects staves of individual instruments (e.g., flute and clarinet; two trumpets; etc.) or multiple vocal parts, whereas the *brace* connects multiple parts for a *single* instrument (e.g., the right-hand and left-hand staves of a piano or harp part).

Brace

A brace is used to connect two or more lines of music that are played simultaneously, usually by a single player, generally when using a grand staff. The grand staff is used for piano, harp, organ, and some pitched percussion instruments. The brace is occasionally called an **accolade** in some old texts and can vary in design and style.

Clefs

A clef assigns one particular pitch to one particular line of the staff on which it is placed. This also effectively defines the pitch range or tessitura of the music on that staff. A clef is usually the leftmost symbol on a staff, although a different clef may appear elsewhere to indicate a change in register. Historically, clefs could be placed on any line on a staff (or even on a space), but modern notation almost exclusively uses treble, bass, alto, and tenor clef.

G clef (Treble clef)

The spiral of a G clef (not a point on the spiral, but the center around which the spiral is drawn) shows where the G above middle C is located on the staff. A G clef with the spiral centered on the second line of the staff is called *treble clef*. The treble clef is the most commonly encountered clef in modern notation.

Alto clef

Tenor clef

C clef (Alto, and Tenor clefs)

The center of a C clef points to the line representing middle C. The first illustration here is centered on the third line on the staff, making that line middle C. When placed there, the clef is called *alto clef*, which is mainly used for the viola but is sometimes used for other instruments. The second illustration shows the clef centered on the fourth line—this clef is called *tenor clef*. Tenor clef is used for bassoon, cello, trombone, and double bass when the notes get very high, avoiding the use of excessive ledger lines.

Until the classical era, C clefs were frequently seen pointing to other lines (it is sometimes called a "movable clef"), mostly in vocal music, but this has been supplanted by the universal use of the treble and bass clefs. Modern editions of music from such periods generally rewrite the original C-clef parts to either treble (female voices), octave treble (tenors), or bass clef (tenors and basses). The C clef was sometimes placed on the third space of the staff (equivalent to an octave treble clef) but this usage is unusual since all other modern clefs are placed on lines.

F clef (Bass clef)

An F clef places the F below middle C on the line between the dots.[2] When placing the F below middle C on the fourth line, as shown here, it is called *bass clef*, which is by far its most common usage. Bass clef appears nearly as often as treble clef in modern music notation. In older notation, particularly for vocal music, F clefs were sometimes centered on the third line (*baritone clef*) but this usage has essentially become obsolete.

Rhythmic values of notes and rests

In American usage, musical note and rest values have names that indicate their length relative to a whole note. A half note is half the length of a whole note, a quarter note is one quarter the length, etc.

Note	British name / American name	Rest
	Large (Latin: Maxima) / Octuple whole note[3]	
	Long / Quadruple whole note[3]	
	Breve / Double whole note	
	Semibreve / Whole note	
	Minim / Half note	
	Crotchet / Quarter note	
	Quaver / Eighth note For notes of this length and shorter, the note has the same number of flags (or hooks) as the rest has branches.	

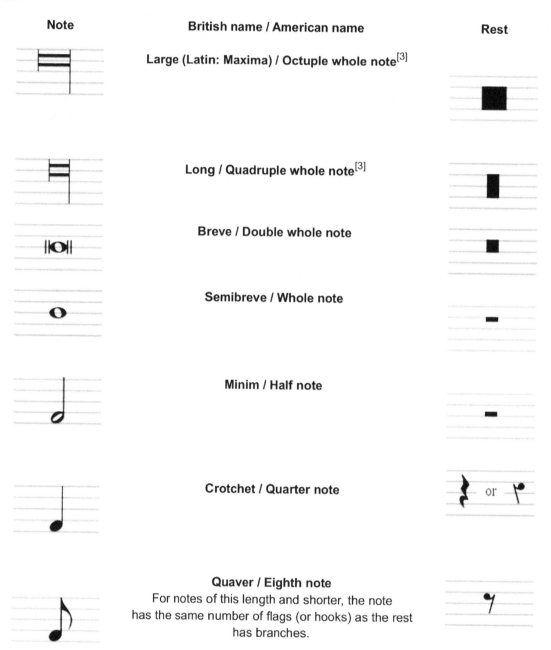

Semiquaver / Sixteenth note

Demisemiquaver / Thirty-second note

Hemidemisemiquaver / Sixty-fourth note

Semihemidemisemiquaver /
Quasihemidemisemiquaver / Hundred twenty-eight
note

Demisemihemidemisemiquaver / Two hundred
fifty-sixth note[]

Beamed notes

Eighth notes (quavers) and shorter notes have flags to indicate their duration, but beams can be used instead of flags to connect groups of these notes. This is usually done to indicate a rhythmic grouping but can also be used to connect notes in ametrical passages. The number of beams is equivalent to the number of flags on the note value—eighth notes are beamed together with a single beam, sixteenth notes with two, and so on. In older printings of vocal music, the use of beams is sometimes reserved for notes that are sung on one syllable of text (melisma). Modern notation of vocal music encourages the use of beaming in a consistent manner with instrumental engraving, however. In non-traditional meters beaming is at the discretion of composers and arrangers and can be used to emphasize a rhythmic pattern.

Dotted note

Placing a dot to the right of a notehead lengthens the note's duration by one-half. Additional dots lengthen the previous dot instead of the original note, thus a note with one dot is one and one half its original value, a note with two dots is one and three quarters—use of more than two dots is rare. Rests can be dotted in the same manner as notes.

Ghost note

A note with a rhythmic value, but no discernible pitch when played. It is represented by a (saltire) cross (similar to the letter x) for a notehead instead of an oval. Composers will primarily use this notation to represent percussive pitches. This notation is also used in parts where spoken words are used.

Multi-measure rest

A compact way to indicate multiple measures of rest. Also called *gathered rest* or *multi-bar rest*.

Breaks

Breath mark

This symbol tells the performer to take a breath (for singers and aerophones) or leave a slight space (for other instruments). This space does not affect the tempo. For instruments that employ a bow, it indicates to lift the bow and start the next note with a new bowing.

Caesura

A pause during which time is not counted.

Accidentals and key signatures

Common accidentals

Accidentals modify the pitch of the notes that follow them on the same staff position within a measure, unless cancelled by an additional accidental.

Flat
Lowers the pitch of a note by one semitone.

Sharp
Raises the pitch of a note by one semitone.

Natural
Renders null a sharp or flat. The sharp or flat may have been indicated as an accidental or defined by the key signature.

Double flat
Lowers the pitch of a note by two semitones. Usually used when the note is already flat in the key signature.[8]

Double sharp
Raises the pitch of a note by two semitones. Usually used when the note is already sharp in the key signature.

Key signatures

Key signatures indicate which notes are to be played as sharps or flats in the music that follows, showing up to seven sharps or flats. Notes that are shown as sharp or flat in a key signature will be played that way in every octave—e.g., a key signature with a B♭ indicates that every B is played as a B♭. A key signature indicates the prevailing key of the music and eliminates the need to use accidentals for the notes that are always flat or sharp in that key. A key signature with no flats or sharps generally indicates the key of C major or A minor, but can also indicate that pitches will be notated with accidentals as required. The key signature examples shown here are as they would appear in treble clef.

Flat key signatures

Sharp key signatures

Time signatures

Most music has a rhythmic pulse with a uniform number of beats—each segment of this pulse is shown as a measure. Time signatures indicate the number of beats in each measure (the top number) and also show what type of note represents a single beat (the bottom number). There may be any number of beats in a measure but the most common by far are multiples of 2 and/or 3 (i.e., 2, 3, 4, and 6). Likewise, any note length can be used to represent a beat, but a quarter note (indicated by a bottom number of "4") or eighth note (bottom number of "8") are by far the most common.

$\dfrac{3}{4}$

Simple time signatures

This example shows that each measure is the length of three quarter notes (crotchets). $\frac{3}{4}$ is pronounced as "three-four" or "three-quarter time".

Compound time signatures

In a compound meter, there is an additional rhythmic grouping within each measure. This example shows $\frac{6}{8}$ time, indicating 6 beats per measure, with an eighth note representing one beat. The rhythm within each measure is divided into two groups of three eighth notes each (notated by beaming in groups of three). This indicates a pulse that follows the eighth notes (as expected) along with a pulse that follows a dotted quarter note (equivalent to three eighth notes).

$\mathbf{C}$

Common time

This symbol represents $\frac{4}{4}$ time—four beats per measure with a quarter note representing one beat. It derives from the broken circle that represented "imperfect" duple meter in fourteenth-century mensural time signatures.

Alla breve or cut time

This symbol represents 2
2 time—two beats per measure with a half-note representing one beat.

Metronome mark

This notation is used to precisely define the tempo of the music by assigning an absolute duration to each beat. This example indicates a tempo of 120 quarter notes (crotchets) per minute. Many publishers precede the marking with letters **"M.M."**, referring to Maelzel's Metronome. This is a tempo marking, not a time signature—it is independent of how the beats are grouped (the top number in a time signature), although it defines the tempo in terms of the counting note (the bottom number).

Note relationships

Tie

When tied together, two notes with the same pitch are played as a single note. The length of this single note is the sum of the time values of the two tied notes. The symbol for the tie and the symbol for the slur appear the same, but a tie can only join two notes of the same pitch.

Slur

While the first note of a slurred group is articulated, the others are not. For bowed instruments this entails playing the notes in a single bow movement, for wind instruments (aerophones) the first note of the slurred group is tongued but the rest of the notes are not—they are played in one continuous breath. On other instruments, like pitched percussion instruments, the notes are connected in a phrase, as if a singer were to sing them in a single breath. In certain contexts a slur may instead indicate that the notes are to be played legato, in which case rearticulation is permitted.

While the slur symbol and the tie symbol appear the same, a tie can only connect exactly two notes of the same pitch; a slur can connect two or more of any pitches. In vocal music a slur normally indicates that notes under the slur should be sung to a single syllable.

A *phrase mark* (or less commonly, *ligature*) is visually identical to a slur but connects a passage of music over several measures. A phrase mark indicates a musical phrase and may not necessarily require that the music be slurred.

Glissando or Portamento

A continuous, uninterrupted glide from one note to the next that includes the pitches between. Some instruments, such as the trombone, timpani, non-fretted string instruments like the cello, electronic instruments, and the human voice can make this glide continuously (portamento), while other instruments such as the piano, harp, or mallet instruments blur the discrete pitches between the start and end notes to mimic a continuous slide (glissando).

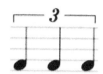

Tuplet

A tuplet is a group of notes that would not normally fit into the rhythmic space they occupy. The example shown is a quarter-note triplet—three quarter notes are to be played in the space that would normally contain two. (To determine how many "normal" notes are being replaced by the tuplet, it is sometimes necessary to examine the context.) While triplets are the most common version, many other tuplets are possible: five notes in the space of four, seven notes in the space of eight, etc. Specific tuplets are named according to the number of grouped notes; e.g., duplets, triplets, quadruplets, etc.

Chord

A chord is several notes sounded simultaneously. Two-note chords are called **dyads**, three-note chords built by using the interval of a third are called **triads**.

Arpeggiated chord

A chord with notes played in rapid succession, usually ascending, each note being sustained as the others are played. It is also called a broken chord, a rolled chord, or an arpeggio.

Dynamics

Dynamics are indicators of the relative intensity or volume of a musical line.

Pianississimo
Extremely soft. Softer dynamics occur very infrequently and would be specified with additional ps.

Pianissimo
Very soft.

_p_

Piano
Soft; louder than _pianissimo_.

_mp_

Mezzo piano
Moderately soft; louder than _piano_.

_mf_

Mezzo forte
Moderately loud; softer than _forte_. If no dynamic appears, _mezzo-forte_ is
assumed to be the prevailing dynamic level.

_f_

Forte
Loud.

_ff_

Fortissimo
Very loud.

fff

Fortississimo
Extremely loud. Louder dynamics occur very infrequently and would be
specified with additional _f_s.

sfz

Sforzando
Literally "forced", denotes an abrupt, fierce accent on a single sound or
chord. When written out in full, it applies to the sequence of sounds or
chords under or over which it is placed. Sforzando is not to be confused with
rinforzando.

_fp_

Fortepiano
Indicates that the note is to be played with a loud attack, and then
immediately become soft.

<

Crescendo
A gradual increase in volume.
Can be extended under many notes to indicate that the volume steadily
increases during the passage.

>

Diminuendo
Also **decrescendo**
A gradual decrease in volume. Can be extended in the same manner as
crescendo.

○, ø, or _n_

Niente
Meaning "nothing". May be used at the start of a crescendo to indicate "start
from nothing" or at the end of a diminuendo to indicate "fade out to nothing".

Rarely, even softer or louder dynamic levels are indicated by adding more **p**s or **f**s. While **ppp** is
called "_pianississimo_" and **_fff_** is called "_fortississimo_", these words (formed by adding an additional
"iss") are not proper Italian.

Dynamics are relative, and the meaning of each level is at the discretion of the performer or the conductor. Laws to curb high noise levels in the workplace have changed the interpretation of very loud dynamics in some large orchestral works, as noise levels within the orchestra itself can easily exceed safe levels.[9]

Articulation marks

Articulations specify the length, volume, and style of attack of individual notes. This category includes accents. Articulations can be combined with one another and may appear in conjunction with phrasing marks (above). Any of these markings may be placed either above or below a note.

Staccato
This indicates that the note should be played shorter than notated, usually half the value, leaving the rest of the metric value silent. Staccato marks may appear on notes of any value, shortening their performed duration without speeding up the music.

Staccatissimo or **Spiccato**
This indicates that the note should be played even shorter than staccato. It is usually applied to quarter notes or shorter notes. In the past this marking's meaning was more ambiguous—it was sometimes used interchangeably with staccato and sometimes indicated an accent and not a shortened note. These usages are now almost defunct but still appear in some scores. For string instruments this indicates a bowing technique in which the bow bounces lightly upon the string.

Tenuto
This symbol indicates that the note should be played at its full value, or slightly longer. It can also indicate a degree of emphasis, especially when combined with dynamic markings to indicate a change in loudness, or combined with a staccato dot to indicate a slight detachment (*portato* or *mezzo staccato*). In percussion notation, this sign indicates a slight accent.

Fermata or Pause
A fermata indicates that a note, chord, or rest is sustained longer than its written value. It will usually appear on all parts in an ensemble. The fermata is held for as long as the performer or conductor desires.

Accent

An accent indicates that a note should be played louder, or with a harder attack than surrounding unaccented notes. It may appear on notes of any duration.

Marcato

A marcato marking indicates that the note should be played louder or more forcefully than a note with a regular accent mark. In organ notation, this sign often does not indicate marcato when in the pedal stave otherwise it still does, but instead that a pedal note should be played with the toe. When printed above the note it indicates the right foot's toe, and below the note indicates the left foot's toe.

Ornaments

Ornaments modify the pitch pattern of individual notes.

Trill

A rapid alternation between the specified note and the next higher note (determined by key signature) within its duration, also called a "shake". When followed by a wavy horizontal line, this symbol indicates an extended, or running, trill. In music up to the time of Haydn or Mozart the trill begins on the upper auxiliary note.[10] In percussion notation, a trill is sometimes used to indicate a tremolo. In French baroque notation, the trill, or *tremblement*, was notated as a small cross above or beside the note.

Upper mordent

Rapidly play the principal note, the next higher note (according to key signature) then return to the principal note for the remaining duration. In some music, the mordent begins on the auxiliary note, and the alternation between the two notes may be extended. (In other words, in some music, the upper-mordent sign means exactly the same as the trill sign.) Regardless of the style of music, the pattern finishes on the principal note. In handbells, this symbol is a "shake" and indicates the rapid shaking of the bells for the duration of the note.

Lower mordent (inverted)

Rapidly play the principal note, the note below it, then return to the principal note for the remaining duration. In much music, the mordent begins on the auxiliary note, and the alternation between the two notes may be extended.

Gruppetto or Turn

When placed directly above the note, the turn (also known as a *gruppetto*) indicates a sequence of upper auxiliary note, principal note, lower auxiliary note, and a return to the principal note. When placed to the right of the note, the principal note is played first, followed by the above pattern. Placing a vertical line through the turn symbol or inverting it, it indicates an *inverted turn*, in which the order of the auxiliary notes is reversed.

Appoggiatura

The first half of the principal note's duration has the pitch of the grace note (the first two-thirds if the principal note is a dotted note).

Acciaccatura

The acciaccatura is of very brief duration, as though brushed on the way to the principal note, which receives virtually all of its notated duration. In some styles of music, the acciaccatura is played exactly on the beat and the principal note is marginally late; in other styles, the acciaccatura is marginally early and the principal note is on the beat. It is also possible on some instruments to play both notes exactly on the beat and then quickly release the acciaccatura. In percussion notation, the acciaccatura symbol denotes the flam, the miniature note still positioned behind the main note but on the same line or space of the staff. The flam note is usually played just before the natural durational subdivision the main note is played on, with the timing and duration of the main note remaining unchanged. Also known by the English translation of the Italian term, **crushed note**, and in German as *Zusammenschlag* (simultaneous stroke).

Octave signs

Ottava alta

8va is placed above the staff to indicate that the passage is to be played one octave higher.

Ottava bassa

8vb is placed below the staff to indicate that the passage is to be played one octave lower.[11][12]

Quindicesima alta

15ma is placed above the staff to indicate that the passage is to be played two octaves higher.

Quindicesima bassa

15^{mb} is placed below the staff to indicate that the passage is to be played two octaves lower.

8va and 15ma are sometimes abbreviated further to *8* and *15*. When they appear below the staff, the word *bassa* is sometimes added.

Repetition and codas

Tremolo

A rapidly repeated note. If the tremolo is between two notes, then they are played in rapid alternation. The number of slashes through the stem (or number of diagonal bars between two notes) indicates the frequency to repeat (or alternate) the note. As shown here, the note is to be repeated at a demisemiquaver (thirty-second note) rate, but it is a common convention for three slashes to be interpreted as "as fast as possible", or at any rate at a speed to be left to the player's judgment.

In percussion notation, tremolos indicate rolls, diddles, and drags. Typically, a single tremolo line on a sufficiently short note (such as a sixteenth) is played as a drag, and a combination of three stem and tremolo lines indicates a double-stroke roll (or a single-stroke roll, in the case of timpani, mallet percussion and some untuned percussion instruments such as triangle and bass drum) for a period equivalent to the duration of the note. In other cases, the interpretation of tremolos is highly variable, and should be examined by the director and performers.

The tremolo symbol also represents flutter-tonguing.

Repeat signs

Enclose a passage that is to be played more than once. If there is no left repeat sign, the right repeat sign sends the performer back to the start of the piece or the movement.

Simile marks

Denote that preceding groups of beats or measures are to be repeated. In the examples here, the first usually means to repeat the previous measure, and the second usually means to repeat the previous two measures. This mark is normally only used in styles of music in which the players commonly expect to play repeated patterns, and in which the mark is therefore frequently encountered; in styles where such a mark would be unusual, repeated measures are written out in full, or the "repeat sign" is used instead.

Volta brackets (1st and 2nd endings, or 1st- and 2nd-time bars)

A repeated passage is to be played with different endings on different playings. Although two endings are most common, it is possible to have multiple endings (1st, 2nd, 3rd ...).

D.C.

Da capo
(lit. "From top") Tells the performer to repeat playing of the music from its beginning. This is usually followed by *al fine* (lit. "to the end"), which means to repeat to the word *fine* and stop, or *al coda* (lit. "to the tail"), which means repeat up to the coda sign and then jump forward into the coda.

D.S.

Dal segno
(lit. "From the sign") Tells the performer to repeat playing of the music starting at the nearest preceding *segno*. This is followed by *al fine* or *al coda* just as with *da capo*.

Segno
Mark used with *dal segno*.

Coda sign
Indicates a forward jump in the music to its coda (ending passage), which is marked with the same sign. Only used after playing through a *D.S. al coda* (Dal segno al coda) or *D.C. al coda* (Da capo al coda).

FineMarks the end of a composition or movement, usually following a repeat command such as D.C. al fine or D.S.

Instrument-specific notation

Bowed string instruments

Left-hand pizzicato or **Stopped note**
A note on a stringed instrument where the string is plucked with the left hand (the hand that usually stops the strings) rather than bowed. On the horn, this accent indicates a "stopped note" (a note played with the stopping hand shoved further into the bell of the horn). In percussion this notation denotes, among many other specific uses, to close the hi-hat by pressing the pedal, or that an instrument is to be "choked" (muted with the hand).

Snap pizzicato
On a stringed instrument, a note played by stretching a string away from the frame of the instrument and letting it go, making it "snap" against the frame. Also known as a Bartók pizzicato.

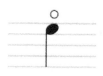

Natural harmonic or Open note

On a stringed instrument, this means to play a natural harmonic (also called **flageolet**). Sometimes, it also denotes that the note to be played is an open string. On a valved brass instrument, it means to play the note "open" (without lowering any valve, or without mute). In organ notation, this means to play a pedal note with the heel (above the note, use the right foot; below the note, use the left foot). In percussion notation this denotes, among many other specific uses, to open the hi-hat by releasing the pedal, or allow an instrument to ring.

Up bow or Sull'arco

On a bowed string instrument, the note is played while drawing the bow upward. On a plucked string instrument played with a plectrum or pick (such as a guitar played pickstyle or a mandolin), the note is played with an upstroke.

Down bow or Giù arco

In contrast to the up bow, here the bow is drawn downward to create sound. On a plucked string instrument played with a plectrum or pick (such as a guitar played pickstyle or a mandolin), the note is played with a downstroke.

Made in the USA
Middletown, DE
07 July 2023

34704901R00097